FLESH, OR MONEY

For Catherine,

Enjoy these poems!

Wes Magee

⌞1996⌟

Wes Magee
Flesh, or Money
POEMS

LITTLEWOOD

Poems © Wes Magee 1990
Published by Littlewood & Arc, The Nanholme Centre,
Todmorden, Lancashire OL14 6DA
Printed by Arc & Throstle Press, Todmorden
Typeset by Anne Lister Typesetting, Halifax

ISBN: 0 946407 55 X

Acknowledgements: These are due to the Editors of the following magazines and journals, in which many of the poems first appeared: *Ambit, Anglo-Welsh Review, 'Contemporary Poets'* (OUP), *Bête Noire, Countryman, Critical Quarterly, Encounter, "New Poetry 6"* (Hutchinson), *New Statesman, Outposts, Poetry Review, Poetry Wales, The Honest Ulsterman, Resurgence, The Literary Review, The Scotsman, 'Stand-points'* (Harrap) and *Tribune*.

Poems also appeared in publications from Priapus Press, or were broadcast on BBC Radio 3 and BBC Radio 4.

FUNDED BY
Lincolnshire & Humberside
ARTS

for Fiona and Peter Ellis

CONTENTS

FOUR

ONE

German measles

In 1945 my mother punched-up the bolster
propping me between starched sheets
while an eiderdown billowed chill
to my chest. Measles had me feverish,
blotched and marasmic. Lugubrious,
the sash-window stood pale with light.
Before me lay piles of 'Picture Post'
and intently I peered at the photographs,
their thousand black dots turning
into blazing tanks, or soldiers with
helmets askew, dead in trenches.

The bedroom door remained shut.
Lino curled toad-cold on the floor.
The wooden bed-ends seemed
like a coffin under construction.
Daily I lapped Virol from a tablespoon
which went down and around and
around an opaque jar of good health.
And the photographs had me frightened,
their blotchy agonies of men and machines
caught in a world as silent and faraway
as the gelid light beyond the tall window.

After the war

It was a July evening, perhaps ten
when he led me to the air-raid shelter,
a blockhouse camouflaged by apple trees
at the end of our long strip of garden.

We crept inside: a swirling cat-blackness,
mattress-damp air, and then his asthmatic rasp
before a tremulous hand touched my blouse.

Outside again . . . the cool dark, insect drone.
We scanned the night's squadron-formation clouds,
saw wing-tip lights of stars filling the sky.
"Listen," he whispered, "listen for the bombs."

I recollected long-drawn whistles, dulled crumps,
heard now apples thudding in the wild grass
as he shook boughs and hared away, whooping.

Through the gloom his searchlight shout, "I love you!"
as from the distant main road there came
the sudden clang of a tram homing in,
kamikaze fashion, on the town centre.

The battlefields

Age twelve I was a Korean War veteran,
my bedroom wall papered with a large-scale
'Geographia' map of the peninsula.
Daily I studied newspaper reports
and marked the front-line with national flags.
I knew each placename and how the war
surged up and down Korea like a rip-tide . . .

The map? – vanished, and faded now those
images of homesick troops, the deep winters,
and tanks abandoned in a wild terrain.
But the names of the battlefields remain, their sharp
syllables more evocative than old newsreels
as I intone them under an English sky
– Pyongyang, Pusan, Seoul, the Yalu river . . .

And beyond Korea the list lengthens,
grows to a global chant one can recite
while driving around a county town,
a liturgy more vivid than war memoirs.
See how densely the markers flag our planet,
each name a wound – Marathon, Crimea, Concord,
Boyne water, Arnhem, the moor at Culloden . . .

Snap

Was it thirty
    years ago
that weekend
    of deep snow

in Germany?
    Ten of us,
conscripts,
    hired a bus

with wheel chains
    and drove north.
The forests alone
    were worth

the trip. Skiing
    brought on collapse:
that, and too much
    pernod, schnapps.

Now my mother
    sends *me* the snap
I sent *her* then:
    a young chap

clean shaven,
    army haircut,
long scarf,
    no hint of a gut.

He stands
    rigid with cold,
nineteen and
    a half years old.

Scrawled on the back:
    "Me in German snow".
Was it thirty
    years ago?

Bucolic

In the broad shade of an oak
view the spread of white linen
set with jugs and bread and fruit.

The noon is laden with heat,
pollen drifts faint from tall grass,
incursions of nettles wilt.

On an upturned pail she sits;
splayed legs, cotton dress, straw hat
– the epitome of summer.

At the river two children
chase crane-flies with muslin nets;
their thin, bare chests rib-shadowed.

When a stone breaks still waters
its splash silvers in the sun,
returns a wealth of ripples,

and by the briary hedge where
cows browse and mooch, a young man
muses on his season's lay.

Above the handkerchiefed head
swallows flit. The air's blue blur
matches the veins beneath his skin.

Teeming insects fuss. The fields
are asway with ripeness as
August perfects her weather.

View this 'ever and always'
when a century stood dazzled
and no cloud ruined the set sky.

Ripe

Across the Wolds
fields are glut with rape,
　　marm rectangles
of sun and butter.

Driving, we gloat
over a landscape
　　gouached in gold:
our ochrous season.

And there, below
muscles of cumulus,
　　harvest's emblem
– a rainbow sharpens.

An Ulster idyll

> Sun
> and clouds compete all day
stippling the fields as stookers
fork sheaves to a heeling wain.
The cob chews in its nosebag
patient for the slow wind home,
straw straggling along green lanes,
blue smoke wisping from steadings.
On blackthorns, linen laid to dry.

> Soon
> the barn's close communion
of beam and mote, propped ladders,
bantams pecking at nothing,
dog tethered near the half-door.
Arm-wrenched the yard pump screeches,
its water twist balm for wrists
grazed and bloodied by stubble.
The gush darkens dusty clogs.

> Soused
> pork and soda bread sate.
Lamps hiss, illume close newsprint
spread wide on a chenille cover.
Tin bath scraping across flags.
Embers in the inglenook.
Now the gloaming's hushed curfew
as night enfolds pool, pasture.
Tick. Tock. Write here, *Ichabod.*

Return to water

At the bridge
boys lie belly-flat on warm planks
and dip for fish. The stream's mirror
gulps their string-held jars.

Trapped minnows
become pike inside glass. One boy
wades downstream, gashes his heel on
a broken bottle.

Touch again
that sun-warmed wood, gaze on blood's bloom
and know once more a seasonal
return to water.

Littoral

The tidemark of clothes
and a teasing breeze,
a zephyr which burns
pate, shank and shoulder.
Sun's silly-ass grin
has everyone stripped;
rites of surf and sand.
Kites ripple, rattle.
Offshore the thud, bounce
of a blue speed-boat.

Observe this woman
prising pliant breasts
into a swimsuit;
another's flop free
with an almost gasp.
That man's past caring;
his pear-drop paunch lolls
over pink-striped pants.
Far down the fried strand
toddlers a-wobble.

Grain by grain the dunes
are trickling inland,
countless voortrekkers
heading for golf links,
margins of salt pools.
Dusk: a mustering
of stumps and sogged dogs.
Litter-lout sea drops
carapaces, kelp,
bones, condoms, dead shags.

TWO

TWO

The love market

Work? We didn't give it a thought!
Jobs were plentiful as apples
but love, ah, that was something else.
At sixteen the need was to find
someone, anyone. Already
snips on the love market were being
snapped up: around town you saw them,
former school-pals going steady,
and never seen Piccadilly!

Yet I'd have given a finger
to gain such status, to link arms
along a sunned strand in summer.
Instead I wintered in fairgrounds
where loudspeakers crackled with rock
but once, lucky, palled with a girl,
walked her down to the dripping bridge.
Shapeless in scarves and duffel coats
we kissed, her lips tight-sealed and dry.
Hearts stammered: words were rare as wrens.

Warmer was the 'Astoria',
a flea-pit where smoke from Woodbines
eddied in the projector's beam,
while from double-seats at the back
sniggers supplemented the soundtrack.
Best was a charabanc trip to
the moors. There gales ruddied pale cheeks
and heather made a springy bed
upon which we lay close and laughed
and swigged flagons of sweet cider.

Suitably it was past midnight
and snowing when, behind a row
of lock-ups, months of fumblings clicked
and her combination of clips
opened. She held an umbrella.
My frozen fingers groped furtive
as the young Michelangelo's!
Days later we entered her house
to conclude the business before
a smouldering fire banked with slack.

* * *

Once more it is winter as I
gaze across the village from this
warm house. Tonight, the stars are set
like studs on a leather jacket,
the moon a curl of orange peel.
In the chapel porch two youngsters
wrestle in the hold of a kiss:
faded denim meets anorak!
Fervent in the frost they sample
goods displayed on the market's stall,

and I think of that long-gone friend
who, young and in love, said, "if God
made anything better then he
kept it for himself." Such rapture
has withered: today work consumes.
Watching these two I envisage
a garden in dark December
where last apples cling to stark trees.
Spurned by birds, shrivelled and palsied
they hang, awaiting the long fall.

Skin flick

Milky cats, the nudes purr,
    slow-stroke legs and breasts
with delicate fingers.
Lips linger long on lips.
Erotic with breathing
    the air swells blue.

Swing doors sigh as you leave.
    In the bare foyer
usherettes stand dumpy
in housecoats. They dandle
torches and suck hard on
    aniseed balls.

Blue movie

Skirt hitched she skeltered across the stream
bounding from boulder to plashed boulder
and where a waterfall poured riches
into a pool lay and cupped and drank
and leaped gasping at such clutch of cold.
Sunlight glanced the *eau de vie* dribbling
down her chin. Startled birds ascended;
glided beyond cornfields.
                    And today,
where does she breathe, among what millions?

This afternoon, the office drowning
in a dismay of memoranda,
certain fall of light unreeled a mood
and that decades-old movie rolled again
in my head.
              It seemed an ancient spar
rose from a sunken ship and surfaced
on a distant ocean, unseen save
for a bird traversing the vast sky,
migrating from brightness into night.

Saturday evenings

Saturday evenings found him
duffel-coated in her front room,
patient while she made her face
before they left for the 'Gaumont',
watching as she stashed lotions,
compact, Buddha-shaped bottles
into a vanity bag which bulged
like the body of a pregnant cat
asleep before a purring fire.

Ritualistic, the shuffling queue
until the cinema's dark claimed them.
On the wide screen Robert Mitchum's ears
were whopping as wheelbarrows.
Amidst the lianas of Craven 'A'
her scent was Atlantic fresh,
and ritualistic their kissing
and cuddling and nuzzling.
Trembling, her hand on his thigh.

She shivered in the bus home.
Petrol fumes made him queasy.
An hour they stood beneath the porch
inarticulate with frustration
until the Yale clicked with finality
and he traipsed home, jelly legged
on the cobbles of that northern town
as Saturday reeled wearily into Sunday.
Decades on her name is a blank,

yet this morning, smoothing lotion
into his cheek after a wet shave,
the vanity bag was recalled.
For a space he stood, immobile
while steam misted on the mirror,
and tried to fix the memory of her face
but it was maddeningly indistinct.
Around him the world grated into first gear;
Saturday morning rituals began.

One cold day

They met and drove through villages
   tucked deep in a crease of England.
October's damp mists blanked out fields.
   Where a roadside river gargled
they parked the car, crossed a mossed bridge
   and dandered around a trout farm,
its meadows pitted with blind pools.

   In each depression fish were crammed
and when fed pellets churned ponds white.
   Hand in gloved hand they meandered
past heaps of netting, rusting tanks,
   hose pipes, then back at the entrance
watched men cudgel rainbow trout and
   pack them for sale in plastic bags.

They left, and later parted where
   they'd earlier made rendezvous.
Dispirited, the clouds hung low:
   a day raw with disaffection.
He drove west, the car's churr a sop.
   In the locked boot three chilled fish lay,
glaucescent eyes fixing the dark.

On Slemish mountain

Paisley's loyalists, I heard,
    lit a bonfire there;
midnight flames of protest
    spiking Antrim's air.
Fifteen years back we climbed
    Slemish, and flesh bare

made sudden, goose-skin love
    on the highest spot.
The sky was a pewter dish
    deep-pitted with shot.
Now a bonfire where we came.
    Remember?
            Or care not?

Mise en scène

Backdrop: night sky, stars,
street lights suspended
like flying saucers.

A darkened bedroom,
velour drapes parted,
wicker chair, cushions.

At the long mirror
a spider holds, shifts
one millimetre.

Lozenges, tablets
on the headboard shelf,
gin in a tumbler

and, mesmeric green,
digital clock glows.
Radiators tick.

Concealed beneath a
tumbled duvet – shoes.
Strewn – bra, tie, trousers.

On the tousled bed
two lie after love
and the scene is set

for tentative words,
lines and dialogue,
a brief kiss, exits.

That other world

Strangers, we gather for a writing course
at a remote country house and discover
there will be no television, newspapers
or radio for the week. Clearly we must
show an interest in each other's problems.
Thankfully, I unwrap whisky in my room.

Our tutor enjoins us to step into
"that . . . that other world . . . the imagination".
He speaks at length of the "creative process".
My piles begin to itch, but the countryside
is rich, and by Day Two we have explored the wood,
forded a river, and scribbled fitfully.

Laughter is heard across fields: someone croons.
A jovial sun joins in the cerebral flush
but night creates a different world of 'other'.
One man strips beneath the stars. In the barn two
figures touch. A lady, seventeen again,
is liberated amidst daisies and grass.

It is like an Iris Murdoch novel;
musical beds more popular than charades.
Too soon it ends. We swop addresses, kiss, and
promise to write. Leaving, I catch cricket scores
on the car radio. Thus another life
intrudes. On the rear seat empty bottles chime.

When?

I think
of that night
in the back
of his car
when stars
overhead
were like
glisks in a bar.
It's days
since we spoke,
now I wait
in the hall.
O when
will he 'phone,
O when
will he call?

I remember
his hands,
his head
on my breast,
the static
that sparked
when he peeled
off his vest.
It was . . .
nothing new
yet his lips
made me moan.
O when
will he call,
O when
will he 'phone?

State

Irritated, I open the front door.
Backlit by street lamps she stands, wide smiling,
            and straightway spouts
an apology. "I know it's late, but . . ."
then spills a loquacious spiel – policies,
pledges, promises and condemnations
of the other lot and all they stand for.
Deaf to her noise I feel expensive heat
rush to perish in chill October's sky.
Across the road the silhouettes of roofs.

While she prates I glower in opposition,
her voice that social glot of manifestos
            and diligent days
spent beavering in committee rooms
decked out with slogan posters, fold-up chairs
and trestle tables set with mugs of tea.
But now her active mouth attracts my gaze,
its gloss-red bow, and so my sight extends
to take in fullness under furs, long legs.
Past the darkened garden a tom cat slinks.

"Well, thank you for your time. We need your vote . . ."
A litho leaflet is passed to my hand
            and for a span
our fingers touch, her skin's freshness a jolt
which starts adrenalin coming in a gush.
She turns on elegant heels. The gate clicks.
In the flow of night air a *frisson* stirs
then dies. From the leaflet a clear-eyed man
looks out, confident, groomed. I scan the blurb
then screw the thing and boot it down the hall.

Next day, driving through town, the election
can't be dodged – favours, vans with placards
            and speakers which
tannoy attention. Idly I glance left
and right for a glimpse of her vivacity
and taste again that strong cocktail – desire
and politics, a mix which has at times
farcically exposed the ambitious
with their pants down. But the day is bleak
and lust shrinks in low temperatures.

More immediate are the precinct punks,
joshing blacks, women bulked against the cold
                    and further out
the car parks, and 'Polling Station' boards wired
to school gates. Windows frame stickers – reds, blues.
Outside a pub a bald man is shouting.
Apolitical I won't vote; a public
duty lost to private affairs, but will
sit till dawn charting swings in *the* big match
then reel to bed and dream of flesh, or money.

THREE

Conference breakfast in Florida

7.10 in the hotel already
and they're into hard sell,
four grafters sporting minty-fresh shirts
          and cologne.
Breakfast done, it's computer predictions
and action-tabbed files as, attentive,
          the alligator skin
                    brief-cases squat.
Air conditioning is citrus scented.

Their talk rate is hard to stomach
as I head down to easy-over eggs,
strips, hash browns, hominy grits, toast
          and jelly.
The coffee's stronger'n coal tar
and there's no avoiding the flight plans,
          figures, contracts, the creative
                    promotional.
Ceiling fans rotate soundlessly.

Oblivious the guys nasal and drawl
while black waiters pad, their red duds
clashing with the colour scheme of things,
          and in truth
I'm witness to early morning devotions,
the day's first prayer station to the dollar.
          Sun's up; warm, yet the palm trees
                    are shivering
and the blue pool wears a goosebump skin.

Reading the limos

From the sidewalk
I'm peering hard
into an Americana
of light reading,
the licence plates
of parked limousines
gaudy with Floridian
county names
– Orange, Palm Beach,
Seminole, Sarasota –
at once sun-drenched
and easy on my
squinty British eye.

And the bumper stickers!
'Baby', 'Gators',
'Another family for
Christ', and 'Honk
if you're horny!'
And yet more
silver pickings,
the metallic scrawls
pinned to tail fins
– Buick, Oldsmobile,
Pontiac, Chevrolet
and Cadillac
Sedan de Ville.

Mouthing all this,
elated, I walk into
a 'New York Times'
vending machine
squatting kerbside
like ArtooDeetoo
and lurch painfully
into the road.
A pick-up truck
screams to a halt.
My t-shirt's narrative
is damage limitation
– 'Don't hit me,

my son's a lawyer'.

Headed for Disney

Orlando, 'the city beautiful',
a syrup blob on the pancake flatness
      of Central Florida,
the city of one hundred new hotels
      spreading way, way out towards Disney.

In a silver Malibu Classic
we slick it down Interstate Four eyeing
      Orlando's helpless sprawl,
the grid of streets saturated with signs,
      all those buy it, buttonholing ads.

Exotic, they sprout; groves of mad growths
in neon, hard-edge, day-glo . . . profusions
      of canvases and boards,
a free pop-art show of the sidewalk hung
      against a backdrop of seamless blue –

Bud, gas, tacos, Wendy's, Kents, Coke, Coors,
cookies. Hey! Today, downtown Orlando
      and headed for Disney
I saw Andy Warhol and Jasper Johns
      and Rauschenberg live in the streets. Hey!

Reciting the placenames in Florida

At a dinner party in the U.S.A.
I was egged on to make a recitation
by Floridians hungry to hear
placenames of the British nation.
    So I held forth
    and found they couldn't get enough
of Blubberhouses, Wetwang and Wildboarclough,
Mankinholes, Oswaldtwistle, Clwyd and Clun,
Muckle Flugga, Mangotsfield and Mannington.

One Sunday, paddling down the Wekiva,
– me, two Yanks, three dames –
Mac bawled as the current swept us along,
"hey, Limey, give us a belt of those names!"
    So I shouted back
    – and they could scarce get their fill –
Moonzie, Capel Curig, Rochester and Rhyl,
Milton Keynes, Yarsop, Yaddlethorpe and Thame,
Galashiels, Gaping Ghyll, Crewe and Dunsinane.

In the Hyatt Hotel, as a speaker droned,
my partner murmured, "this is *shit*!
Let's hear those placenames.
Come on, Wes, hit us with them, Brit!"
    So I stood up
    and cleared my throat with a loud och,
let rip with March, Machynlleth, Dundee, Dolgoch,
Llanelli, Llandrillo, Tolpuddle, Tycoch,
Aberdeen, Achnasheen, Aike and Abersoch,
and Llanfairpwllgwyngyllgogerychwynbwlllantisiliogogogoch!

Groggy

Too, too late your wry assessment,
"she's something of a bar-room brawler,"

as after dawn I weaved back to my apartment,
groggy, wiping sawdust from my eyes.

Hallucinogenically a red cardinal
started to warble in a kerbside palm

and the automatic sprinklers all came on,
misting the pavement. I knelt to drink,

sluiced a taproom taste from my throat
while my desert boots darkened, darkened.

Veteran

Over eggs benedict in the coffee shop
I read a slogan fading on the back
of his windcheater – *Together then,*
Together again – his vets. chapter
a decade, a continent
        out from Vietnam.

Sideburns greying, his faraway look
mirrors your eyes at the dinner party
when thoughtlessly I brought up
'the War'. Knives chimed on silence
as you and the others were back
        in student days –

the sixties, marches, buttons and banners,
headband guerrillas in heartland U.S.A.
It seemed I'd traced a cold finger
along scar tissue, touched a wound
yet tender, and now must
        watch you wince.

So it is I *know* his quiet,
the hunched back, the way
he flips quarters to the formica
like spent cartridges clattering on baked mud,
how he shoulders the door
        and is gone.

Cold, the eggs lie. Sense with me
that moment after the door swung shut,
the empty space, and a desolation
hidden deep within a nation.
I sensed it then, and writing this
        do so again.

Western

A rough-neck, saddle-sore and but one mile
ahead the sheriff's posse, a growing
dust-cloud back there in the arid landscape.
He has no choice but to ride hard until
his mare folds, lungs raw. Then the mercy shot
        echoing through distant hills.

Now he sprawls in a rock's shade and waits for
the future to arrive. Sweat stiffens his
shirt. Time enough to recall the beatings,
his father's absence, and that girl who took
the stage-coach east: signs which led him blind to
        this heat-stunned, waterless place.

Excuses are hollow consolations
and how merciless the sun's righteous glare.
When the grim-faced avengers come, hauling
on reins, rifle barrels straight as the law,
there is his cracked-smile surrender, relief
        that at last it is over.

Elvis: The poem

Bounty hunter
from my far West
he gyrated
into TV town
and holed up at
Heartbreak Hotel,
the guitar-slinger
with a lip sneer
for whom madams
and molls grew moist
at a wriggle of
his little finger.

Eds and Ellas frowned,
others thumped Bibles
as he cleaned up in
Nashville's saloons
where no one rolled
a hip faster.
On every wall
his name and mug-shot
– the most wanted man,
before fast food,
ice-cream soddened him.
Tears on Boot Hill.

Best remember
the lanky kid
casual against a
gas pump in Memphis
while, behind him, the
pick-up truck idles.
On its front seat
an old strum box
warming in the day,
and climbing sky-high
the sun's gold disc
not yet in his sights.

Coincidental
a found poem

President Lincoln
was elected in 1860,
Kennedy in 1960.

Their successors
were both named Johnson.
Andrew being born in 1808,
Lyndon in 1908.

Booth, Lincoln's killer
was born in 1839.
Oswald in 1939.

Both men
were assassinated
before their trials.

Lincoln's secretary,
named Kennedy,
advised him not to go
to the theatre.

Kennedy's secretary,
named Lincoln,
pressed him not to go
to Dallas.

Booth shot Lincoln
in a theatre
and ran into a warehouse.

Oswald shot Kennedy
from a warehouse
and ran into a theatre.

Where were you?

Bill had cut-up a novel
cons were rotting inside
    the scent of joss
    was strong in the doss
the day Jack Kennedy died

Dogs devouring a postman
chickens gutted and fried
    hands hearts and holes
    arriving in shoals
the day Jack Kennedy died

Snow had shrouded the graveyard
frost was kissing the bride
    give her full due
    she went right through the crew
the day Jack Kennedy died

Phil got up for the first time
two in bed and both cried
    rock 'n' roll beat
    was fagged on its feet
the day Jack Kennedy died

Skulls lay grinning in junk shops
mouths were opening wide
    cancer and pain
    and flesh down the drain
the day Jack Kennedy died

No idea where I was, pet
mem'ries gone with the tide
    when out of the blue
    a named bullet flew
the day Jack Kennedy died

'No teenage crime was recorded during the Beatles appearance on the Ed. Sullivan Show in 1964, in the U.S.A.'

We're all home
no more liqor store
    watching
the Beatles
    in 1964.

Sheath that shiv
punks against the law
    cruising
the airwaves
    in 1964.

Spook the rich
finger-lickin' poor
    filching
the hand-outs
    in 1964.

Jo loves John
read it on the shore
    surfing
the white caps
    in 1964.

Daddy-o
caught us in the raw
    pulling
our plonkers
    in 1964.

I love you
roll me on the floor
    getting
a feel up
    in 1964.

John Paul George
Ringo out to score
    goosing
the groupies
    in 1964.

Uncle Sam
soon we're off to war
    dreaming
of Vietnam
    in 1964.

Rip it up!
Man, this *is* a bore
    watching
the Beatles
    in 1964.

Waiting for dinner while the chairperson speaks

Literally a redneck,
florid in Florida,
his Southern drawl
lulls the mike
to snooze point
while we sit,
rumbling with hunger
on the fifth floor
of this plush hotel.

The iced water serves
to hone appetites
but meantime
he's into another
wearisome wisecrack:
"Ah sed t'Bob
thar's a nip in th'air
and Bob sez,
whal les drink it!"

He mimics my slur
last night in the Langford,
crucified after four
'Rusty Nail' cocktails,
yet now he staggers
into an in-com-pre-
hen-sible story about
Winston Churchill
and a chicken.

Glazed, my gaze
floats from this fastness,
across Lake Eola
to its floodlit
Centennial Fountain
– a quadruple scoop
of mint-choc ice-cream
wobbling on a
tarnished silver plate.

Girl in the ice-cream parlour

Across town a freight train is sounding
     its organ-tuning warnings
as I step from the sidewalk's dead heat
into a cool parlour, its red-white gleam
     clean as a fresh-cut apple

where, "whal'll ya have?" throws me,
     as does the red-visored girl.
My "ice-cream, please," sounds feeble.
"Whal . . . we gadit!" and she indicates
     illuminated boards

listing everything from crushed cranberries
     to cashews and boorsteyvants.
Conscious of my confusion she prepares
a mélange of melon ice, syrup,
     walnut lumps and thick cream,

a castle of confection, then quips
     "ah jus adore ya necktah!"
Rich, I sit in the window, spooning,
while she sings along with a country station,
     her voice a pure sound

and I'm charmed by an unblemished beauty.
     Together we inhabitat
an harmonious world even as, outside,
bronzed skateboarders rattle past,
     swirling the day's dust and warmth.

FOUR

After a prison visit: Hull

for A. S. Byatt

The outer door closed: we stood in the street,
in drizzle; a cinematic cliché.
    Inside, hardmen were being banged up:
ping-pong, snooker tables mustering dust.
Hull was abed early as, heads lowered,
we made for the car . . . the wind and the rain . . .

One hour on we were downing malts, trebles,
in the lounge bar of a swanky hotel
    thoughts yet with the lags, the lifers
in that cramped room, their peck-order questions
about writing, the boisterous atmosphere
which shut down when you read from your novel,

its elegance captivating cons who
grew rapt, wide-eyed as a class of Infants.
    For a spell, release; and snout smoke
coiling slow around the lovers' narrative.
Then a prepared public-school parody –
the vote of thanks, applause, beefy handshakes.

Whisky anaesthetised that experience;
logs spat. MacCaig, seventy, loosed his word hoard.
    It was three when I reached my room,
glopped at fleeing clouds. The stars were wire lights
for our planet clink, the moon's watchtower probe
restless, cold over field and barn and copse.

Hauling back the blankets a stale must swarmed,
sour mnemonic for that stir's air, recycled
    through the thousand lungs, tubercular.
Still it's with me, that hour, recalled each time
I bend to pot the black and sniff the baize's stour
or hear ping-pong's wasteful sound – wronged, wrong,

        wronged, wrong,
        wronged, wrong.

Before the Bench, 1864

The day
after Gala
and Fanny Hanson, wobbly grogged,
is up before the Bench
charged with burglariously breaking into
the Station Master's
house.

Nosegays,
phials of salts
dispel her fish-gutting-shed stench.
Blained and carbuncular
she hugs her wrap of rags then blabs, yammers
incoherently:
hawks.

She is
declared insane:
on Monday conveyed to Lincoln,
the asylum whose inmates blench
when oak doors slam out light. Her life is doused;
a tallow candle,
snuffed.

Cover

A small tradition, I take my son
to view the waxworks as my parents
took me. In the Chamber of Horrors
we trudge from Hitler to Charles Manson.
One grim tableau pulls a crowd: Christie
the mass killer of Rillington Place
papering-over a wall-cupboard
inside which one of his victims hangs.

I remember how, as a school boy,
I furtively read of Christie's murders,
the macabre midnight burials.
Now, as then, his bland gaze and cheap specs
serve to conceal a brain swarming with
destructions, and I understand his
need to cover up that fatal flaw,
show a blameless visage to the world.

Balding, frail, Christie stands spectral pale
in this house of wax. Silenced, we stare,
sensing in him a fleshed-out image
of all the deaths we've wished on others.
My boy whines, impatient to move on.
Outside we greet friends, laugh in the sun,
cover with smiles as wide as wallpaper
the skull's dingy cupboard hung with hurt.

Domestic prisons

1. The cooker

The Nazi cooker holds a chicken in solitary
and even though electrified circuits foil escape
    the prisoner is trussed and skewered.
Adaptable, the cooker doubles as crematorium:
just sniff that flesh sizzling in the oven.

2. The cupboard

Beneath the stairs, in a wedge-shaped cupboard,
shoes are incarcerated in black-hole conditions.
    Daily the captives march to work.
At night they return to a stifling darkness,
thinner, worn out, sodden with sweat.

3. The sink

The kitchen sink is a gulag of greasy water
and here the table's undesirables are dumped.
    Hot water torture is common practice;
mugs are brain-washed, glasses crack,
and slimy plates swiftly spill the beans.

Still in the enemy camp

after William Wantling

"Listen, this estate's a no-go landscape.
Yesterday, we're in the precinct, right,
when some punks called me Longhair
and took the piss out of Jenny's shawl.
One yob crapped, "carry your bag, sir?"
and, "what's it like humping your Granny?"
You know, those shitkickers tracked us
to the pad and made with the aggro.
They were plugged into the electric soup
and when they bricked us the windows
surrendered. That brought the filth running.
Now the night hangs in here like cold, man.
We're through with these confrontations,
I mean, we've blown it, you know?
This is a tight-assed hole and no way,
no way you can be laid back.
So we're cutting loose, hitting the road,
moving on from this zilch to wherever,
but for sure clear of this gagaland.
So, no more shooting the shit,
spill it man, where can we find
          the least fucked-up enemy camp?"

Incident on the housing estate

Day long the lamps diffuse orange light.
From one a bicycle tyre hangs. Mongrels,
macho curs of the precinct, roam in packs.
Set deep among the regiments of homes
a corner shop stands adrift in litter,
its flagstoned forecourt stained with spilled cola,
the grass verge threadbare. Here two youths battle,
vicious and blatant, scattering shoppers.

I stop the car and order them to part.
One flings a "fuck off out of it", then fells
his opponent, slams knees on a thin chest.
Mucus swings from his nose like nylon string
as he batters the boy's face before they
roll, rise, and run flailing amidst traffic.
They part, hurling abuse cruel as their fists.
Thunder raindrops of blood stipple the flags.

I drive away, shaken, seeing anew
this vast estate where I have worked for years:
the weary pre-cast housing, gardens grey
and useless, the squads of shouting children.
A punctured space hopper lies dead in a
gutter. Crude sex is spelled out on the walls.
Evening hauls down steel shutters and street lamps
droop with shame. That we have come to this,
$$\text{this.}$$

A scene

Crepuscular, the day dies:
a Polack danders with his sable chow,
   another leans on his gate
   while in the hedge sparrows clown.
The men nod, swop syllables:
     one looks up the street,
       the other down.

Pan . . . an Eastern-bloc drabness
fags the estate. Skins frig in a shelter,
   their kick-your-skull demeanour . . .
Yamaha (trans: stuff you Jack)
throttles in view, the rider
   unidentified,
     sexless in black.

A flash, and its shriek snaps.
Glissading bike prangs the shelter, takes skins,
   men, voiding dog, hedge and gate.
   All leans here; birds scorch the place.
Opaque visor holds the scene,
     lunar-like scape on
       the biker's face.

In the betting shop: South London

No club smoking-room this
although phlegm-yellow fug
    nicotines the ceiling.
Emulsioned walls are spread
with sheets from 'Sporting Life'
    and signs: 'No Spitting'.

The punters, men, some old,
lean on a narrow shelf
    and agonise a quid
on *Hill of Slane* or one
that fell the last time out.
    Favourites are not favourite.

Behind an ornate grille
a girl defines boredom,
    doles winnings from rolled wads
of greasy notes. Young blacks
parody themselves with shouts
    of "shit, man!", hands-down slaps.

Some hold the littered floor
and watch the race-board where
    a man scratches his rocks
then pens weights, odds, withdrawals.
The on-course lineman comes
    tight-lipped from the squawk-box.

For two minutes – tension:
the "get ons", fast breathing,
    the fists stuffed into jeans,
the pocket billiards.
It ends – this weekday wank –
    in self-disgust and groans.

Yet, oke to flutter time
off streets, away from kids
  ·   half-wild on building sites,
the wife's demands and wants,
to idle afternoons
    in rituals, small delights.

Thoughtful between races
they await the lineman,
      their link with paddock, beer
in the Grandstand bar, silks,
lush grass and winning post,
      those acres of fresh air.

Cries of London

the busker and his echoes in the subway
    the fans wild-singing on the train
  the mugged girl weeping in the precinct
    the rain

the marchers and their banner-calls for justice
    the juke-box belting through the bars
  the old jane cursing in the washroom
    the cars

the hoardings with their claims and scarlet language
    the crazed drunk yelling out his fears
  the news-stands brash and bold with headlines
    the tears

the dancers as they fall out from the disco
    the weirdo beat up by the boys
  the wet streets filled with feet and voices
    the noise.

Imagine

"It must be twenty years since we last met;
then it was beads, bells and going braless.
        It all seems so long ago . . .
When the children came it meant Chippenham
and here we are; quiet place, no police.
This room's wonderfully sunny; upstairs
we've tenants. The back garden's overgrown
but at least we live well on nettle soup!
Cats? Hairy Krishna and Jackson. Jackson?
You remember . . . Angela Davis' boy friend.
        Recalls it all, doesn't it?
Kind of you to bring a bottle. It will
go down well with Rupert's curry and beans.
He stays home, reading mostly: at present
it's Musil's 'A man without qualities'.
I earn . . . social work . . . half the time people
        don't turn up for interview.
The children are Chet and Shane. Today they're
barefoot around the house but come Monday
it's toe-the-line for the Primary school
even if those CND badges on
their Fairisles *do* look incongruous next
to Gnasher and old Dennis the Menace.
Help yourself, but watch the 'fridge. Vomits its
contents as soon as you open the door.
Lavatory's back there. Lennon's picture
on the wall . . . dark glasses, big fedora . . .
nice one. Never tire of him . . . *'imagine*
there's no heaven, it's easy if you try' . . .
We still dream the peaceful revolution.
        Remember when we hitched up
the A1, that rock concert in Leicester?
The first time we'd seen anyone topless.
Then it was all togetherness: flowers
        from 'Frisco to Felixstowe!
Right now I feel the children shoving me
to one side and everything's turning grey.
Later I have to read a paper on
council housing at the ward meeting. Bind.
More rosy than red these days, I suppose.
Flabbergasted to get your call. *You've* not
        changed much. So tell me, how's things?"

61

About the Author

WES MAGEE was born in Greenock, Scotland, in 1939, and after leaving school at 15 worked as a bank-clerk before doing National Service in West Germany. Between 1965 and 1968 he attended Goldsmith's College, University of London. Until recently he was a primary school headmaster near York. Now he has left to become a freelance writer. He is well-known as an author for children as well as adults. This is his fourth full-length collection of adult poetry. His second, 'No Man's Land', was a Poetry Book Society Recommendation.